D1277177

SAYINGS OF POOR RICHARD

From Poor Richard's Almanack

By
BENJAMIN FRANKLIN

FLEMING H. REVELL COMPANY

Westwood, New Jersey

Library of Congress Catalog Card Number: 60–13099

Printed in the United States of America

1.1

INTRODUCTION

Many men have written treatises on how to attain health, wealth, success, and long life. Benjamin Franklin is one of the few who reached what he preached.

Son of a Boston soapmaker—the fifteenth of seventeen children—young Ben left school at ten to help his father and then to work for a half brother as printer's devil. Moving to Philadelphia in his teens, he was not long in opening his own printing shop. In 1732, the year George Washington was born, Franklin began publishing *Poor Richard's Almanack.*

Of the thirteen books published in Philadelphia in one year, seven were almanacs; they were the best-sellers of colonial America. But Poor Richard's edition, mixing proverbs and doggerel with the usual meteorological and astronomical predictions, outsold the competition at the rate of 10,000 copies a year for twenty-six years.

At the age of forty-two Franklin retired from publishing to devote the rest of his eighty-four years to science and the public service. "The wisest American" seems a felicitous description of the man who invented the lightning rod, proposed a plan of union for the Thirteen Colonies, helped draft the Declaration of Independence, represented the new nation abroad, and contributed substantially to the establishing of the Constitution.

A sampling of his wit and wisdom is in the pages that follow, printed as faithfully as possible in the style of the original. Many of Poor Richard's sayings were re-worked from various sources, but all bear the unmistakable stamp of "B. Franklin, Printer."

Some of Poor Richard's philosophy seems as quaint as the ancient spelling. Thrift, hard work, saving for a rainy day, moderation in diet, wariness toward debt: these are not watchwords of the twentieth century. One wonders whether some of them may be in the twenty-first; whether the best of Poor Richard is not so much outgrown as ahead of us, waiting for us to sense its perennial wisdom.

THE PUBLISHERS

SAYINGS OF POOR RICHARD

I. Friendship

A true Friend is the best Possession.

> An open Foe may prove a curse;
> But a pretended Friend is worse.

Friendship increases by visiting Friends, but by visiting seldom.

When befriended, remember it: When you befriend,—forget it.

The rotten Apple spoils his Companion.

'Tis great Confidence in a Friend to tell him your Faults, greater to tell him his.

If you would keep your secret from an enemy, tell it not to a friend.

Tart words make no Friends: spoonful of honey will catch more flies than Gallon of Vinegar.

Now I have a Sheep and a Cow, every Body bids me Good morrow.

The same man cannot be both Friend and Flatterer.

A Brother may not be a Friend, but a Friend will always be a Brother.

Be slow in chusing a Friend, slower in changing.

When a Friend deals with a Friend,
Let the bargain be clear and well penn'd,
That they may continue Friends to the End.

Friends are the true Sceptres of Princes.

Promises may get thee friends, but non-performance will turn them into enemies.

Beware of meat twice boil'd, and an old Foe reconciled.

Thou can'st not joke an Enemy into a Friend, but thou may'st a Friend into an enemy.

Monkeys, warm with envious spite, their most obliging friends will bite.

The wise Man draws more advantage from his Enemies, than the Fool from his Friends.

No better relation than a prudent and faithful friend.

Thus still should private Friendships spread around,
Till in their joint Embrace the Publick's found,
The common Friend!—Then all her Good explore;
Explor'd, pursue with each unbias'd Power
But chief the greatest should her Laws revere,
Ennobling Honours, which she bids them wear
Ambition fills with Charity the Mind,
And pants to be the Friend of all Mankind.

It is better to take many Injuries, than to give one.

Fish and visitors smell in three days.

Hear no ill of a friend, nor speak any of an enemy.

There are three faithful friends—an old wife, an old dog, and ready money.

A false Friend and a Shadow attend only while the Sun shines.

To be intimate with a foolish Friend, is like going to Bed to a Razor.

Be civil to all; sociable to many; familiar with few; Friend to one; enemy to none.

Friendship cannot live with Ceremony, nor without Civility.

Lend money to an enemy, and thou'lt gain him; to a friend, and thou'lt lose him.

Love your Neighbor; yet don't pull down your Hedge.

It is generally agreed to be Folly, to hazard the loss of a Friend, rather than to lose a Jest. But few consider how easily a Friend may be thus lost. Depending on the known regard their Friends have for them, Jesters take more Freedom with Friends than they would dare to do with others, little thinking how much deeper we are wounded by an Affront from one we love. But the strictest Intimacy can never warrant Freedoms of this Sort; and it is indeed preposterous to think they should; unless we can suppose Injuries are less Evils when they are done to us by Friends, than when they come from other Hands.

II. Concerning Time

Employ thy time well, if thou meanest to gain leisure.

Dost thou love life? Then do not squander Time; for that's the Stuff Life is made of.

Lose no time. Be always employed in something useful. Cut off all unnecessary actions.

Since thou art not sure of a Minute, throw not away an Hour.

You may delay, but Time will not.

Time enough always proves little enough.

Prodigality of Time produces Poverty of Mind as well as of Estate.

If you have time, don't wait for Time.

One To-day is worth two To-morrows.

To-morrow never comes.

Haste makes Waste.

Leisure is Time for doing something useful; this Leisure the diligent man will obtain, but the lazy man never.

Trouble springs from Idleness, and grievous Toil from needless Ease.

To-morrow every Fault is to be amended; but that To-morrow never comes.

To-morrow you'll reform, you always cry;
In what far country does this morrow lie,
That 'tis so mighty long ere it arrive?
Beyond the *Indies* does this morrow live?
'Tis so far-fetched this morrow, that I fear
'Twill be both very old, and very dear.
To-morrow I'll reform, the fool does say;
To-day itself's too late;—the *wise* did yesterday.

Let all your things have their places. Let each part of your business have its time.

An egg to-day is better than a hen to-morrow.

He that riseth late, must trot all day, and shall scarce overtake his business at night.

He that resolves to mend hereafter, resolves not to mend now.

Make haste slowly.

There's a time to Wink as well as to see.

Each year one vicious habit rooted out,
In time might make the worst man good throughout.

Time is an herb that cures all diseases.

Lost time is never found again.

Wish a Miser long life, and you wish him no good.

Ah simple Man! when a boy two precious jewels were given thee, Time and good Advice; one thou hast lost, and the other thrown away.

A STRIKING SUNDIAL

How to make a STRIKING SUNDIAL, by which not only a Man's own Family, but all his Neighbours for ten Miles round, may know what a Clock it is, when the Sun shines, without seeing the Dial.

Chuse an open Place in your Yard or Garden, on which the Sun may shine all Day without any Impediment from Trees or Buildings. On the Ground mark out your Hour Lines, as for a horizontal Dial, according to Art, taking Room enough for the Guns. On the Line for One o'Clock, place one Gun; on the Two o'Clock Line two Guns, and so of the rest. The Guns must all be charged with Powder, but Ball is unnecessary. Your Gnomon or Style must have twelve burning Glasses annex't to it, and be so placed that the Sun shining through the Glasses, one after the other, shall cause the Focus or burning Spot to fall on the Hour Line of One, for Example, at One a Clock, and there kindle a Train of Gunpowder that shall fire one Gun. At Two a Clock, a Focus shall fall on the Hour Line of Two, and kindle another Train that shall discharge two Guns successively: and so of the rest.

Note, There must be 78 Guns in all. Thirty-two Pounders will be best for this Use; but 18 Pounders may do, and will cost less, as well as use less Powder, for nine Pounds of Powder will do for one Charge of each eighteen Pounder, whereas the Thirty-two Pounders would require for each Gun 16 Pounds.

Note also, That the chief Expense will be the Powder, for the Cannon once bought, will, with Care, last 100 Years.

Note moreover, that there will be a great Saving of Powder in Cloudy Days.

Kind Reader, Methinks I hear thee say, That is indeed a good Thing to know how the Time passes, but this Kind of Dial, notwithstanding the mentioned Savings, would be very Expensive; and the Cost greater than the Advantage, Thou art wise, my Friend, to be so considerate beforehand; some Fools would not have found out so much, till they had made the Dial and try'd it. . . . Let all such learn that many a private and many a publick Project, are like this Striking Dial, great Cost for little Profit.

III. As to the Weather

WEATHER PREDICTIONS

. . . among the multitude of our astrological predictions, 'tis no wonder if some few fail; for, without any defect in the art itself, 'tis well known that a small error, a single wrong figure overseen in a calculation, may occasion great mistakes: But, however we Almanack-makers may *miss it* in other things, I believe it will generally be allowed *that we always hit the day of the month*, and that I suppose is esteem'd one of the most useful things in an Almanack.

As to the weather, if I was to fall into the method my brother J——n sometimes uses, and tell you, *Snow here, or in New-England,—Rain here, or in South Carolina,—Cold to the northward,—Warm to the southward*, and the like, whatever errors I might commit, I should be something more secure of not being detected in them: But I consider it will be of no service to any body to know what weather it is 1000 miles off, and therefore I always set down positively what weather my reader will have, to be where he will at the time. We modestly desire only the favorable allowance of *a day or two before, and a day or two after* the precise day against which the weather is set;—and if it does not come to pass accordingly, let the fault be laid upon the printer, who, 'tis very like, may have transposed or misplac'd it, perhaps for the conveniency of putting in his holidays: and since, in spight of all I can say, people will give him great part of the credit of making my Almanacks, 'tis but reasonable he should take some share of the blame.

HOW TO SECURE HOUSES, &C. FROM LIGHTNING

It has pleased God in his Goodness to Mankind, at length to discover to them the Means of securing their Habitations and other Buildings from Mischief by thunder and Lightning. The Method is this: Provide a small Iron Rod (it may be of the Rod-iron used by the Nailors) but of such a length, that one End being three or four Feet in the moist Ground, the other may be six or eight Feet above the highest Part of the Building. To the upper end of the Rod fasten about a Foot of Brass Wire, the size of a common Knitting-needle, sharpened to a fine Point; the Rod may be secured to the House by a few small Staples. If the House or Barn, be long, there may be a Rod and Point at each End, and a middling Wire along the Ridge from one to the other. A house thus furnished will not be damaged by Lightning, it being attracted by the Points, and passing thro' the Metal into the Ground without hurting anything. Vessels also, having a sharp pointed Rod fix'd on the Top of their Masts, with a Wire from the Foot of the Rod reaching down, round one of the Shrouds, to the Water, will not be hurt by Lightning.

IV. Shillings, Groats, & Pounds

HOW TO GET RICHES

The Art of getting Riches consists very much in Thrift. All Men are not equally qualified for getting Money, but it is in the Power of every one alike to practice this Virtue.

He that would be beforehand in the World, must be beforehand with his Business: It is not only ill Management, but discovers a slothful Disposition, to do that in the Afternoon, which should have been done in the Morning.

Useful Attainments in your Minority will procure Riches in Maturity, of which Writing and Accounts are not the meanest.

Learning, whether Speculative or Practical, is, in Popular or Mixt Governments, the Natural Source of Wealth and Honour.

Light purse, heavy heart.

For Age and Want save while you may;
No morning Sun lasts a whole Day.

A rich rogue, is like a fat hog, who never does good til as dead as a log.

He's a Fool that makes his Doctor his Heir.

Make no expense but to do good to others or yourself; i.e., waste nothing.

He's gone, and forgot nothing but to say *Farewell* to his creditors.

Rather go to bed supperless than run in debt for a Breakfast.

Lying rides upon debt's back.

Creditors have better memories than Debtors.

He that sells upon Trust, loses many friends, and always wants money.

Borrowing makes sorrowing.

A good Wife & Health, is a Man's best Wealth.

He that pays for work before it's done, has but a pennyworth for two pence.

If you'd lose a troublesome Visitor, lend him money.

He who buys had need have 100 Eyes, but one's enough for him that sells the Stuff.

Great Spenders are bad Lenders.

The poor have little,
Beggars none;
The rich too much
Enough not one.

He who multiplies Riches multiplies Cares.

Beware of little Expenses: a small leak will sink a great Ship.

The creditors are a superstitious sect, great observers of set Days and Times.

Pay what you owe, and what you're worth you'll know.

'Tis hard (but glorious) to be poor and honest: An empty Sack can hardly stand upright; but if it does, 'tis a stout one!

Wealth is not his that has it, but his that enjoys it.

He that is of Opinion Money will do every Thing may well be suspected of doing every Thing for Money.

All things are cheap to the saving, dear to the wasteful.

The thrifty maxim of the wary Dutch, is to save all the money they can touch.

Not to oversee Workmen, is to leave them your Purse open.

Money & Man a mutual Friendship show:
Man makes false Money, Money makes Man so.

If your Riches are yours, why don't you take them with you to the t'other World?

A little house well fill'd, a little field well till'd, and a little wife well will'd, are great riches.

Who is rich? He that rejoices in his Portion.

If you'd know the Value of Money, go and borrow some.

If worldly Goods cannot save me from Death, they ought not to hinder me of eternal Life.

> Avoid dishonest gain; no price,
> Can recompence the pangs of vice.

If you'd be wealthy, think of saving, more than of getting: The Indies have not made Spain rich, because her Outgoes equal her Incomes.

Wealth and Content are not always Bed-fellows.

The second Vice is Lying, the first is running in Debt.

Better is a little with content than much with contention.

V. Of Foolish Controversy

Men differ daily, about things which are subject to Sense, is it likely then they should agree about things invisible?

When you're good to others, you are best to yourself.

A quarrelsome Man has no good Neighbours.

Neglect kills Injuries, Revenge increases them.

In other men we faults can spy,
And blame the mote that dims their eye;
Each little speck and blemish find;
To our own stronger errors blind.

Avoid extremes. Forbear resenting injuries so much as you think they deserve.

Write Injuries in Dust, Benefits in Marble.

Is there anything men take more pains about than to make themselves unhappy?

He is a Governor that governs his Passions, and he a Servant that serves them.

When Knaves betray each other, one can scarce be blamed or the other pitied.

Love your Enemies, for they tell you your Faults.

Don't throw stones at your neighbours', if your own Windows are glass.

Doing an Injury puts you below your Enemy; Revenging one makes you but even with him; Forgiving it sets you above him.

Quarrels never could last long,
If on one side only lay the wrong.

'Tis more noble to forgive, and more manly to despise, than to revenge an Injury.

Many a long dispute among Divines may be thus abridg'd, It is so: It is not so, It is so; It is not so.

Those who in Quarrels interpose,
Must often wipe a bloody Nose.

Honest Men often go to Law for their Right; when Wise Men would sit down with the Wrong, supposing the first Loss least. In some Countries, the Course of the Courts is so tedious, and the Expence so high, that the Remedy, *Justice*, is worse than *Injustice*, the Disease. In my Travels I once saw a Sign call'd *The Two Men at Law;* One of them was painted on one Side, in a melancholy Posture, all in Rags, with this Scroll, *I have lost my Cause.* The other was drawn capering for Joy, on the other Side, with these Words, *I have gain'd my Suit;* but he was stark naked.

VI. Good Health and Long Life

Tolerate no uncleanliness in body, clothes, or habitation.

To lengthen thy Life, lessen thy Meals.

He's the best physician that knows the worthlessness of the most medicines.

Early to Bed and early to rise,
Makes a Man healthy, wealthy, and wise.

Eat few Suppers, and you'll need few Medicines.

Use now and than a little Exercise a quarter of an Hour before Meals, as to swing a Weight, or swing your Arms about with a small Weight in each Hand; to leap, or the like, for that stirs the Muscles of the Breast.

They that study much, ought not to eat so much as those that work hard, their digestion being not so good.

God heals, and the Doctor takes the Fees.

Many Dishes, many Diseases.

Eat to live, and not live to eat.

If thou would'st live long, live well; for Folly and Wickedness shorten life.

We are not so sensible of the greatest Health as of the least Sickness.

Wish not so much to live long, as to live well.

An infallible Remedy for *Toothache*, viz.—Wash the root of an aching Tooth, in *Elder vinegar*, and let it dry half an hour in the Sun; after which it will never ache more.

He that would travel much, should eat little.

I saw few die of hunger; of eating—100,000.

'Tis easier to suppress the first Desire, than to satisfy all that follow it.

A fat kitchen, a lean will.

Eat not to dullness. Drink not to elevation.

Nothing more like a Fool, than a drunken Man.

Time eateth all things, could old Poets say;
The Times are chang'd, our times *drink* all away.

A full Belly makes a dull Brain.

When the Wine enters, out goes the Truth.

He that never eats too much, will never be lazy.

9 Men in 10 are suicides.

He that spills the Rum loses that only; He that drinks it, often loses both that and himself.

If thou eatest so much as makes thee unfit for Study, or other Business, thou exceedest the due Measure.

VII. As to Speaking

The Wit of Conversation consists more in finding it in others, than showing a great deal yourself. He who goes out of your Company pleased with his own Facetiousness and Ingenuity, will the sooner come into it again. Most men had rather *please* than *admire* you, and seek less to be *instructed* and *diverted*, than *approved* and *applauded*, and it is certainly the most delicate Sort of Pleasure, to *please another*.

But that sort of *Wit*, which employs itself insolently in Criticizing and Censuring the Words and Sentiments of others in Conversation, is absolute *Folly;* for it answers none of the Ends of Conversation. He who uses it neither *improves others*, is *improved* himself, or pleases any one.

Half Wits talk much but say little.

Words may shew a man's Wit, but Actions his Meaning.

Man's tongue is soft,
And bone doth lack;
Yet a stroke there with
May break a man's back.

Here comes Glib-Tongue: who can out-flatter a Dedication; and lie, like ten Epitaphs.

Praise little, dispraise less.

The heart of the fool is in his mouth, but the mouth of the wise is in his heart.

Tongue double, brings trouble.

Speak not but what may benefit others or yourself. Avoid trifling conversation.

A soft Tongue may strike hard.

As we must account for every idle Word, so we must account for every idle Silence.

When you speak to a man, look on his eyes; when he speaks to thee, look on his mouth.

Three may keep a secret, if two of them are dead.

If you have no Honey in your Pot, have some in your Mouth.

A pair of good Ears will drain dry an hundred Tongues.

Silence is not always a Sign of Wisdom, but Babbling is ever a Folly.

Great talkers should be crop'd, for they have no need of ears.

He's a Fool that cannot conceal his Wisdom.

Teach your child to hold his tongue, he'll learn fast enough to speak.

Approve not of him who commends all you say.

Better slip with foot than tongue.

None preaches better than the ant, and she says nothing.

Here comes the orator with his flood of words, and his drop of reason.

Mary's mouth costs her nothing, for she never opens it but at others' expense.

He that speaks much, is much mistaken.

Many a Man's own Tongue gives Evidence against his Understanding.

Clearly spoken, Mr. Fogg! You explain English by Greek.

Speak and speed: the close mouth catches no flies.

Tell a miser he's rich, and a woman she's old, and you'll get no Money of one, nor Kindness of t'other.

A Slip of the Foot you may soon recover,
But a Slip of the Tongue you may never get over.

Proclaim not all thou knowest, all thou owest, all thou hast, nor all thou can'st.

None are deceived, but they that confide.

There's small revenge in words, but words may be greatly revenged.

Speak with contempt of none, from slave to king,
The meanest Bee hath, and will use, a sting.

You may talk too much on the best of Subjects.

To whom thy secret thou dost tell,
To him thy Freedom thou dost sell.

Since I cannot govern my own tongue tho' within my own teeth, how can I hope to govern the tongues of others?

When man and woman die,
As poets sung
His heart's the last part moves,
Her last, the tongue.

VIII. Diligence & Industry

Plough deep while Sluggards sleep, and you shall have Corn to sell and to keep.

The Cat in Gloves catches no Mice.

The Day is short, the Work great, the Workmen lazy, the Wages high, the Master urgeth; Up, then, and be doing.

God gives all Things to Industry.

Little Strokes,
Fell great Oaks.

Drive thy Business, or it will drive thee.

The sleeping Fox catches no Poultry. Up! Up!

If you'd have done, Go: If not, send.

Industry pays Debts, Despair encreases them.

Have you somewhat to do to-morrow; do it to-day.

God helps them that help themselves.

Up, sluggard, and waste not life; in the Grave will be sleeping enough.

Well done, is twice done.

For want of a Nail the Shoe is lost; for want of a Shoe the Horse is lost; for want of a Horse the Rider is lost.

He that hath a Trade, hath an estate.

Diligence is the mother of good luck.

There are lazy minds as well as lazy bodies.

No man e'er was glorious, who was not laborious.

The busy Man has few idle Visitors; to the boiling Pot the Flies come out.

Trouble springs from Idleness; Toil from Ease.

Laziness trots so slowly that Poverty soon overtakes him.

She that will eat her breakfast in her bed,
And spend the morn in dressing of her head,
And sit at dinner like a maiden bride,
And talk of nothing all day but of pride,
God in his mercy may do much to save her,
But what a case is he in that shall have her.

Be always ashamed to catch thyself idle.

No Gains without Pains.

O Lazy bones! Dost thou think God would have given thee arms and legs, if he had not design'd thou should'st use them?

Sloth (like Rust) consumes faster than Labour wears; and used Key is always bright.

Keep thy shop, and thy shop will keep thee.

A life of leisure and a life of laziness are two things.

Idleness is the Dead Sea, that swallows all Virtues: Be active in Business, that Temptation may miss her Aim; The Bird that sits, is easily shot.

All things are easy to Industry, all things difficult to Sloth.

'Tis easy to frame a good bold resolution;
But hard is the Task that concerns execution.

OF HONEST EMPLOYMENT

It is observable that God has often called Men to Places of Dignity and Honour, when they have been busy in the honest Employment of their Vocation. *Saul* was seeking his Father's Asses, and *David* keeping his Father's Sheep, when called to the kingdom. The Shepherds were feeding their Flocks, when they had their glorious Revelation. God called the four Apostles from their Fishery, and *Matthew* from the Receipt of Custom; *Amos* from among the Horsemen of *Tekoah*, *Moses* from keeping *Jethro's* Sheep, *Gideon* from the *Threshing Floor*, etc. God never encourages Idleness, and despises not Persons in the meanest Employments.

IX. To Live Jollily

Fear to do ill, and you need fear nought else.

Wrong none by doing injuries or omitting the benefits that are your duty.

> Seek Virtue, and of that possest,
> To Providence resign the rest.

Tricks and treachery are the practice of fools that have not wit enough to be honest.

Use no hurtful deceit. Think innocently and justly; if you speak, speak accordingly.

Fear not death; for the sooner we die, the longer we shall be immortal.

'Tis easier to prevent bad Habits than to break them.

He that lies down with Dogs, shall rise up with fleas.

If you would reap Praise you must sow the Seeds,
Gentle Words & useful Deeds.

Learn of the skilful: He that teaches himself, hath a fool for his master.

There is much difference between imitating a good man, and counterfeiting him.

In a discreet man's mouth a publick thing is private.

If you do what you should not, you must hear what you would not.

Bad Gains are truly Losses.

To be content look backward on those who possess less than yourself, not forward on those who possess more.

Who pleasure gives, shall joy receive.

An honest Man will receive neither Money nor Praise that is not his due.

Prayers and Provender hinder no journey.

He that can have Patience can have what he will.

Fly Pleasures, and they'll follow you.

Be not disturbed at trifles or at accidents common or unavoidable.

Observe all men; thyself most.

He is ill clothed that is bare of virtue.

Virtue may not always make a Face handsome, but Vice will certainly make it ugly.

He that lives carnally, won't live eternally.

> There is neither honour nor gain,
> Got in dealing with a vil-lain.

What more valuable than Gold? Diamonds. Than Diamonds? Virtue.

Innocence is its own Defence.

To err is human, to repent divine; to persist devilish.

The excellency of Hogs is—fatness; of Men—Virtue.

A little well-gotten will do us more good,
Than lordships and scepters by Rapine and
Blood.

Virtue & Happiness are Mother & Daughter.

There is no Man so bad but he secretly respects the Good.

How many observe Christ's Birth-day! How few his Precepts! O! 'tis easier to keep Holidays than Commandments.

You may be more happy than Princes, if you will be more virtuous.

Who is strong? He that can conquer his bad
Habits.
Who is rich? He that rejoices in his Portion.

What you would seem to be, be really.

It's the easiest Thing in the World for a Man to deceive Himself.

A good Example is the best Sermon.

Keep thou from the Opportunity, and God will keep thee from the sin.

Great beauty, great strength, and great riches are really and truly of no great use; a right Heart exceeds all.

What is serving God? 'Tis doing Good to Man.

Girls, mark my Words; and know, for Men of Sense,
Your strongest Charms are native Innocence.
Shun all deceiving Arts; the Heart that's gain'd
By Craft alone, can ne'er be long retain'd.
Arts on the Mind, like paint upon the Face,
Frights him, that's worth your Love, from your Embrace.
In simple Manners all the Secret lies
Be kind and virtuous, you'll be blest and wise.

Mankind are very odd Creatures: One half censure what they practise, the other half practise what they censure; the rest always say and do as they ought.

Many have quarrel'd about Religion, that never practised it.

'Tis easy to see, hard to foresee.

If thou dost ill, the joy fades, not the pains;
If well, the pain doth fade, the joy remains.

Liberality is not giving much, but giving wisely.

Enjoy the present hour, be mindful of the past; & neither fear nor wish the approaches of the last.

Life with Fools consists in Drinking;
With the wise Man, Living's Thinking.

What maintains one Vice would bring up two children.

If you would not be forgotten, as soon as you are dead and rotten, either write things worth reading, or do things worth the writing.

A Man has no more Goods than he gets Good by.

Sell not virtue to purchase wealth, nor liberty to purchase power.

Duty is not beneficial because it is commanded, but is commanded because it is beneficial.

Pardoning the Bad, is injuring the Good.

None but the well-bred Man knows how to confess a fault, or acknowledge himself in an error.

If Passion drives, let Reason hold the Reins.

Be not niggardly of what costs thee nothing, as courtesy, counsel, and countenance.

Think of three Things, whence you came, where you are going, and to whom you must account.

Well done is better than well said.

Retirement does not always secure Virtue; Lot was upright in the City; wicked in the Mountain.

Be at War with your Vices, at Peace with your Neighbours, and let every New-Year find you a better Man.

The noblest question in the world is, *What good may I do in it?*

Do not do that which you would not have known.

Sin is not hurtful because it is forbidden, but it is forbidden because it is hurtful.

Would you live with ease, do what you ought, not what you please.

Trust thyself, and another shall not betray thee.

Anger is never without a Reason, but seldom with a good One.

Resolve to perform what you ought. Perform without fail what you resolve.

Search others for their Virtues, thyself for thy Vices.

Keep Conscience clear,
Then never fear.

He that can compose himself, is wiser than he that composes books.

An ill Wound, but not an ill Name, may be healed.

Well, my friend, thou art just entering the last Month of another year. If thou art a Man of Business, and of prudent Care, be like thou wilt now settle thy accounts, to satisfy thyself whether thou hast gain'd or lost in the Year past, and how much of either, the better to regulate thy future Industry or thy common Expenses. This is commendable—But it is not all.—Wilt thou not examine also thy *moral* Accompts, and see what improvements thou hast made in the Conduct of Life, what Vice subdued, what Virtue acquired; how much *better*, and how much wiser, as well as how much richer thou art grown? What shall it *profit* a Man, if he *gain* the whole World, but *lose* his own Soul. Without some Care in this Matter, tho' thou may'st come to count thy thousands, thou wilt possibly still appear poor in the Eyes of the Discerning, even *here*, and be really so for ever *hereafter*.

Let no pleasure tempt thee, no profit allure thee, no ambition corrupt thee, no example sway thee, no persuasion move thee, to do any thing which thou knowest to be evil; so shalt thou always live jollily: for a good conscience is a continual Christmas.

X. Common Sense

Good Sense is a Thing all need, few have, and none think they want.

Where Sense is wanting, Everything is wanting.

Fools need Advice most, but only wise Men are the better for it.

A good Wife lost is God's gift lost.

He that's content hath much. He that complains has too much.

Men & Melons are hard to know.

Doors & walls are fools paper.

No wood without bark.

Anoint a villain and he'll stab you, stab him, and he'll anoint you.

Snowy winter, a plentiful harvest.

Visits should be short, like a winters day,
Lest you're too troublesom hasten away.

Willows are weak, but they bind the Faggot.

A house without woman and firelight, is like a body without soul or sprite.

Little Rogues easily become great Ones.

Kings & Bears often worry their keepers.

A Child thinks 20 Shillings and 20 Years can scarce ever be spent.

Old Boys have their Playthings as well as young Ones; the Difference is only in the Price.

Nothing dries sooner than a Tear.

Great Estates may venture more; Little Boats must keep near Shore.

Beware of the young Doctor & the old Barber.

You may be too cunning for one, but not for all.

He has chang'd his one ey'd horse for a blind one.

Let thy Child's first lesson be obedience, and the second will be what thou wilt.

He that hath no Ill-Fortune will be troubled with Good.

A Change of Fortune hurts a wise Man no more than a Change of the Moon.

To bear other people's afflictions, every one has courage and enough to spare.

At 20 years of age the will reigns; at 30 the wit; at 40 the judgment.

Write with the learned, pronounce with the vulgar.

Those who have nothing to be troubled at, will be troubled at nothing.

If evils come not, then our fears are vain;
And if they do, fear but augments the pain.

The Wise and Brave dares own that he was wrong.

The Proud hate Pride—in others.

Rob not for burnt offerings.

He that speaks ill of the Mare, will buy her.

Pray don't burn my House to roast your Eggs.

Nothing brings more Pain than too much Pleasure; nothing more bondage than too much Liberty, (or Libertinism).

You will be careful, if you are wise;
How you touch men's Religion, or Credit,
or Eyes.

He that scatters thorns, let him not go barefoot.

Late Children, early Orphans.

Good wives and good plantations are made by good Husbands.

Ben beats his Pate, and fancys wit will come;
But he may knock, there's nobody at home.

Don't judge of Men's Wealth or Piety, by their Sunday Appearances.

Ill Customs & bad Advice are seldom forgotten.

Men meet, mountains never.

When Knaves fall out, honest Men get their goods: When Priests dispute, we come at the Truth.

Kate would have Thomas, no one blame
her can:
Tom won't have Kate, and who can blame
the Man?

Death takes no bribes.

One good Husband is worth two good Wives; for the scarcer things are the more they're valued.

Never praise your Cider or your Horse.

Hunger never saw bad bread.

There is no little enemy.

You may sometimes be much in the Wrong, in owning your being in the Right.

Distrust & caution are the parents of security.

A Farmer once made a Complaint to a
Judge,
My Bull, if it please you, Sir, owing a
Grudge,
Belike to one of your good Worship's
Cattle,
Has slain him out-right in a mortal Battle:
I'm sorry at heart because of the Action,
And want to know how must be made Satis-
faction.
Why, you must give me your Bull, that's
plain
Says the Judge, or pay me the Price of the
Slain.
But I have mistaken the Case, Sir, says *John*,
The dead Bull I talk of, & please you, 's my
own:
And yours is the Beast that the Mischief
has done.
The Judge soon replies with a serious Face:
Say you so; then this Accident *alters the
Case.*

You may give a Man an Office, but you cannot give him Discretion.

He that has not got a Wife, is not yet a compleat Man.

My Love and I for Kisses play'd,
She would keep stakes, I was content,
But when I won she would be paid.
This made me ask her what she meant:
Quoth she, since your are in this wrangling vein,
Here take your Kisses, give me mine again.

A lean Award is better than a fat Judgment.

There are three Things extreamly hard, Steel, a Diamond and to know one's self.

Poverty, poetry, and new titles of honour, make men ridiculous.

The painful Preacher, like a candle bright,
Consumes himself in giving others Light.

God works wonders now and then; Behold! a lawyer, an honest man.

Most People return small Favours, acknowledge middling ones, and repay great ones with Ingratitude.

Visit your Aunt, but not every Day; and call at your Brother's, but not every night.

Blessed is he that expects nothing, for he shall never be disappointed.

Beware, beware! he'll cheat 'ithout scruple, who can without fear.

Many a Man would have been worse, if his Estate had been better.

Keep your eyes wide open before Marriage, half shut afterwards.

Content and Riches seldom meet together,
Riches take thou, contentment I had rather.

Many a Man thinks he is buying Pleasure, when he is really selling himself a Slave to it.

Let all Men know thee, but no man know thee thoroughly: Men freely ford that see the shallows.

God, Parents, and Instructors, can never be requited.

Experience keeps a dear school, yet Fools will learn in no other.

When the well's dry, we know the worth of water.

There are no ugly loves, nor handsome prisons.

Hear Reason, or she'll make you feel her.

Many complain of their Memory, few of their Judgment.

Meanness is the Parent of Insolence.

Honours change manners.

Printers . . . should be very careful how they omit a Figure or a Letter: For by such means sometimes a terrible Alteration is made in the Sense. I have heard, that once, in a new Edition of the *Common Prayer*, the following Sentence, *We shall all be changed in a Moment in the twinkling of an Eye:* by the Omission of a single Letter, became *We shall all be hanged in a Moment*, &c. to the no small Surprise of the first Congregation it was read to.

The Morning Daylight appears plainer when you put out your Candle.

Those who are fear'd, are hated.

All Blood is alike ancient.

The things which hurt, instruct.

Let thy discontents be thy secrets;—if the World knows them 'twill despise thee and increase them.

The Eye of the Master, will do more than his Hand.

Don't go to the Doctor with every distemper, nor to the Lawyer with every quarrel, nor to the Pot for every thirst.

Clean your Finger, before you point at my Spots.

Hope and a Red-Rag are Baits for Men and Mackerel.

Laws like to cobwebs, catch small flies,
Great ones break through before your eyes.

The Horse thinks one thing, and he that saddles him another.

Light heel'd Mothers make leaden heel'd Daughters.

Would you persuade, speak of interest, not of reason.

Don't think to hunt two Hares with one Dog.

He that pursues two Hares at once, does not catch one and lets t'other go.

He that would catch Fish, must venture his Bait.

The worst wheel of the cart makes the most noise.

It is wise not to seek a Secret and honest not to reveal it.

The doors of Wisdom are never shut.

An undutiful Daughter will prove an unmanageable Wife.

In Rivers and bad Governments, the lightest Things swim at top.

The learned Fool writes his Nonsense in better Language than the unlearned; but still 'tis Nonsense.

The Sting of a Reproach is the Truth of it.

EPITAPH ON A WORTHY CLERGYMAN

Still like his Master, known by breaking Bread,
The Good he entertained, the needy fed;
Of Humour easy, and of Life unblam'd,
The Friend delighted, while the Priest reclaim'd.
The Friend, the Father, and the Husband gone,
The Priest still lives in this recording Stone;
Where pious Eyes may read his Praises o'er,
And learn each Grace his Pulpit taught before.

The good or ill hap of a good or ill Life, is the good or ill choice of a good or ill Wife.

Craft must be at charge for clothes, but Truth can go naked.

As honest *Hodge* the Farmer sow'd his
Field,
Chear'd with the Hope of future Gain
'twould yield,
Two upstart Jacks in Office, proud and vain,
Come riding by, and thus insult the Swain:
You drudge and sweat, and labour here,
Old Boy,
But we the Fruit of your hard Toil enjoy.
Belike you may, *quoth Hodge,* and but
your Due,
For, Gentlemen, 'tis HEMP I'm sowing
now.

He that won't be counsell'd, can't be help'd.

Half the Truth is often a great Lie.

To all apparent beauties blind
Each blemish strikes an envious mind.

Love well, whip well.

He that cannot obey, cannot command.

The Golden Age never was the present Age.

Seven wealthy towns contend for Homer dead,
Thro' which the living Homer beg'd his bread.

Sudden Pow'r is apt to be insolent, sudden Liberty saucy; that behaves best which has grown gradually.

A flatterer never seems absurd:
The flatter'd always takes his word.

Nothing humbler than Ambition, when it is about to climb.

A Mob's a Monster; Heads enough but no Brains.

Grief often treads
  Upon the heels of pleasure,
Marry'd in haste,
  We oft repent at leisure;
Some by experience
  Find these words misplaced,
Marry'd at leisure,
  They repent in haste.

Two dry Sticks will burn a green One.

Let thy maid-servant be faithful, strong, and homely.

Declaiming against Pride, is not always a Sign of Humility.

There was never a good knife made of bad Steel.

Forewarn'd, forearm'd.

How few there are who have courage enough to own their Faults, or resolution enough to mend them!

Talking against Religion is unchaining a Tyger; the Beast let loose may worry his Deliverer.

Cut the Wings of your Hens and Hopes, lest they lead you a weary Dance after them.

Why does the blind man's Wife paint herself?

If Jack's in love, he's no Judge of Jill's Beauty.

He that builds before he counts the Cost, acts foolishly; and he that counts before he builds, finds that he did not count wisely.

The discontented Man finds no easy Chair.

The Bell calls others to Church, but itself never minds the Sermon.

Glass, China, and Reputation, are easily crack'd, and never well mended.

Where yet was ever found the mother, who'd change her booby for another?

If man could have Half his Wishes, he would double his Troubles.

Great Good-nature, without Prudence, is a great Misfortune.

Philosophy as well as Foppery often changes Fashion.

Men take more pains to mask than to mend.

Success has ruin'd many a Man.

The honey is sweet, but the Bee has a Sting.

Tim was so learned, that he could name a Horse in nine Languages. So ignorant, that he bought a Cow to ride on.

Bad commentators spoil the best of books,
So God sends meat (they say) the Devil Cooks.

You can bear your own Faults, and why not a Fault in your Wife.

Hide not your Talents, they for Use were made.
What's a Sun-Dial in the Shade?

I pray Heav'n defend these Colonies from every enemy; and give them bread enough, peace enough, money enough, and plenty of good cyder.

> Reader farewel, all Happiness attend thee;
> May each New-Year, better and richer find
> thee.